Cryptocurrency

The Ultimate Guide to Cryptocurrencies and Digital Money; Learn about Blockchain and How to Invest in Bitcoin, Ethereum, Litecoin and More

Table Of Contents

Cryptocurrency 1

Table Of Contents 2

Introduction..3

Chapter 1: What is Cryptocurrency? 5

Chapter 2 : What Are The Advantages of Using Cryptocurrency? 9

Chapter 3 Types of Cryptocurrency and Uses: – Bitcoin, Ethereum, Litecoin and Other Forms of Altcoin 17

Chapter 4 : Legitimacy of Cryptocurrency 30

Chapter 5: Blockchain.. 36

Chapter 6 : How Cryptocurrency Works in Practice- – Buying Through Exchange Platforms 42

Chapter 7: Investments in Cryptocurrency 49

Chapter 8: Digging for Victory- A Chapter on Mining 55

Chapter 9: Wallets 61

Chapter 10: Case Studies – Three Examples of Investors in Cryptocurrency- Who Made Good 65

Conclusion 69

Introduction

Thank you for taking the time to download this book: Cryptocurrency by Charles Hamilton.

An Encouraging Tale

Let us start with the story of Jered Kenna. In 2010 Mr. Kenna was one of the early pioneers of Bitcoin use. He bought 5000 coins of the new currency for the modest price of 20 cents each – so a total outlay of $1000. Although not an insignificant sum, nevertheless a speculative amount to spend.

Then, in a fit of presumed forgetfulness, he wiped his computer clean, eliminating 800 of these coins forever. Not overly concerned at the time, today his error would cost him, or any other equally forgetful soul, in the region of £2 million - or not far short of $3million.

Mind you, his foresight in buying the currency would mean that the remaining 4200 coins are worth upwards of a cool $14 million at the time of writing. Not a bad return?

What is This Book About?

In this book, you should learn about cryptocurrency – that is Bitcoin and all the other global digital currencies that populate the internet. We hope that you will discover about the uses and advantages of crypto currencies, reasons for their success and, - occasionally -

the risks associated with the various types of digital currency. These risks are sometimes real, more often simply perceived from media driven misinformation.

You should gain a background into the context of these new ways to invest and trade, and learn about blockchain – the technology on which cryptocurrencies are built. Super secure, private, public (the two opposites are not oxymoronic in the case of cryptocurrency), and truly democratic in that it is a technology and operating platform controlled by its users.

With a context in which to understand the new phenomena, you will learn how to acquire your own cryptocurrency, how to store it and how to use it.

In thanking you for choosing this book, I hope that you find it extremely useful as an introduction to an exciting, growing and potentially highly profitable global financial development.

Once again, thanks for downloading this book, I hope you find it to be helpful!

Chapter One: What is Cryptocurrency?

Evolution is a natural process on Earth. It is seen in the development of life beginning from bacteria, through to simple cell organisms, to complex animals, mammals, apes, and eventually human form. We can see evolution just as naturally in the journey the words such as you are now reading have taken. From the earliest oral history and tales, through the beginnings of books, to words written painstakingly by hand on finest velour.

Thomas Caxton's invention of the printing press ensured a sudden surge forward, and who would have envisaged, even thirty years ago, that people would happily read books online or store their entire library on a paperback size piece of slim, lightweight technology?

We could be experiencing the same sense of evolution with the emergence of crypto currency. From earliest barter, through payment with goods of worth, physical coinage linked to gold and fiat currency methods to pay for goods and services have developed to meet the needs of their users. Until, finally, we moved on to exchange rates to cope with international trade, credit cards, and internet banking. We are entering a point of history where cryptocurrency is emerging as a substantial conduit for trade.

What Exactly Is Cryptocurrency?

In its easiest terms, cryptocurrency is digital money. The currency itself is represented by a series of encrypted codes that possess monetary worth. No problem about carrying the weight of pocketsful of coins, even if this is often the term used to describe this currency, your money exists in a line of numbers.

Just as there are many different physical currencies in the world, so there are many cryptocurrencies. These include the original form, Bitcoin, and, in no order, Auroracoin, Dash, Monero, Bitconnect, Namecoin, Burstconnect, Zcash, Vertcoin, Primecoin, Ubiq and the interestingly named Titcoin.

We will look in more detail at some of these currencies later in the book.

What Are The Similarities and Differences Between Physical Currencies and Cryptocurrency

While traditionally most currencies have a hard cash form, we are moving increasingly towards the online use of these monies. Dollars, Sterling, the Euro, etc., most nations have their own type of currency. To illustrate the point, we can consider, for example, salaries. These days, salaries are mostly paid directly to bank accounts. For even longer, the tax has been removed for most at the source and is never actually handled. We only physically see and touch our money when we take it out of the bank. In the context of this, a move to where there is no physical existence of the currency, nothing you can hold, remove from your pocket, and feel the clink of change is not so unexpected.

We trade using debit and credit cards – checks are already on their last legs, how much longer before cash joins them, constrained to the pages of school history books and museum displays? Smaller Tap and Go payments do not even need authorization. So, one significant similarity is that both forms of currency exist (at least in part for physical currencies) in digital form.

Another similarity is that both types are potentially subject to taxation and regulation when used for services, or as payment for work rendered. The USA has issued clear guidance for the use of cryptocurrencies. It says that any person or organization that creates any form of convertible currency, which is virtual, is liable under the existing law once that currency is used as payment or sale to another. However, a difference also exists here – the taxation of cryptocurrency is, at present at least, normally theoretical, while physical and fiat currencies are subject to actual taxation. In many parts of the world, there is yet no taxation. We will consider when and how this might change later in the book.

Like pre-existing currencies in global use, cryptocurrencies have a value that is usable in most parts of the world. There are a few exceptions. Iceland does not accept cryptocurrency, and nor does Vietnam. While the form is legal in China and Russia, these nations impose severe restrictions on its use.

Beyond that, the use of cryptocurrency is (at the time of writing) viable throughout the world.

In addition to the difference that you cannot keep cryptocurrency in your pocket and hand it over to pay for a chocolate bar, receiving your change from the shopkeeper, there are two major differences between traditional currencies and cryptocurrencies.

The first of these is that the value of cryptocurrencies is entirely separate from the influence of Government. While national organizations may affect the value of its fiat currency against others, for example by imposing tariffs or restricting as well as increasing supply; cryptocurrency value is dependent on its global use.

Connected to this is the second major difference. For most cryptocurrency, there is a cap on production and hence supply. Therefore, the market will be limited by this cap. While, for example, a country can produce more currency by simply printing it (called quantitive easing, and an inflationary device) there will be, to quote the largest and most recognizable form, only a limited number of bitcoins will be in circulation. The value of these coins will increase or decrease over time, but there will always be a finite figure on the number of available for digital use.

Chapter Two: What Are The Advantages of Using Cryptocurrency?

In this section, we will look at some of the strongest arguments in favor of the use of cryptocurrency. But, as with all the best things in life, there are some caveats to consider as well. These do need to be regarded in the context of the many benefits – real and potential – this currency type offers. After all, just because drinking too much excellent red wine might cause a headache, that is not a reason to disregard it entirely.

Drinking that Claret with an understanding of its effects means that you can get the benefits but be aware of any risks.

World Wide Currencies

With the exceptions of the nations mentioned in the earlier chapters, crypto currencies are global sources of money. When paying for goods or services from overseas by traditional methods, customers (that is you and I) are subject to the vagaries of interest rates, the whims of Government tariffs and such like. Cryptocurrencies exist in isolation from these limitations and restrictions and are therefore simpler to use and clearer regarding their value.

Simplicity of Use

As the transfer is a simple digital process, it is a very straightforward one. Connected to this (and explored further in the next point) the transaction does not involve a middle man. Banks, credit cards and agencies such as PayPal all charge a fee in some form or other to facilitate your use of your money. Sometimes this will be a straight transaction charge, at other times it will be in the form of interest or as a part of a wider tranche of charges.

Transactions are also instant. Monies are not held up (as by, for example, a bank or more often an escrow agent such as Paypal), and so delays are avoided.

Also, digital money is, well, digital. It can be used as and when the owner wishes. Often, with traditional banking methods, money can be tied up for long periods.

A final point in this area is that it is harder to get into financial difficulties using crypto currency, since users can only spend what they own.

Transactions Remain the Sole Business of the Parties Directly Involved

A cryptocurrency transaction takes place between just the sender and receiver of the payments. There is no middle man involved. Not only does this have the benefit of removing any commission fee, but it also maintains privacy. Cryptocurrency exchanges are based on a PUSH mechanism, which means that only the sum agreed is requested, no other information is required. By contrast, bank transfers, credit card usage and so on all include an element of description for a transaction. Thus, information about the business is available to third parties.

While this does not apply to cash trade, the practicalities of paying by cash are often much more challenging than digital trade, especially when larger payments are involved. For example, security, distance, and exchange rates all combine to make a cash deal more complicated than other forms of trading.

Security is Strong

Using blockchain (another element of digital trading we will examine in more detail later) permanent records of transactions exist, although they remain the business of just the sender and receiver.

The chip-wallet in which cryptocurrencies are stored by most are more secure than a physical wallet, debit card or credit card which can be lost or more easily hacked.

More than this, an account can only be used by the owner. Because everything is preserved and recorded online, suspicious activities are easily spotted, and accounts can then be blocked. Once the authentic user has been informed, and the problem resolved, then the account becomes active once more.

Typical credit card providers, especially banks, are becoming increasingly adept at identifying suspicious activities on accounts, and they then follow a similar procedure to that identified above. However, there is usually a delay between the questionable use and the report to the account owner, and during that time we become vulnerable to either costs or a heavy hassle procedure to resolve the problem.

Transactions undertaken through use of cryptocurrency are untraceable and cannot be reclaimed. This again ensures the security of transfer and ease of use.

Inflation-Proof Accounting and Freedom from Government Interference

Because cryptocurrency is not linked to national currencies, and therefore is not subject to political interference, the money we own is protected from inflation. Owners have the confidence to know that the value of their account regarding its purchase power remains constant.

While taxation is still a slightly gray area at present, transactions using digital currencies are not usually subject to Government legislation – where they are, tracing details is much more difficult, leaving users to act on their own honesty in reporting profits where proper and necessary.

A Sound Investment

Papers regularly report stories of internet users whose bitcoins (or other currencies) are now worth a small fortune. Those who have taken the plunge to make use of cryptocurrency have seen the value of their money increase when compared to existing physical currencies.

So far, there is little indication that this trend will not continue. Indeed, in the short term, with established financial institutions looking to expand their role in digital currency, values may increase further.

Flexibility of Use

As with all innovations, one of the initial difficulties with owners of Bitcoin (the first cryptocurrency) was that it was new, and therefore not widely used. With a move towards increasingly widespread application for everyday services (for example, paying for insurance) and the likelihood of mainstream institutions becoming much more involved in the use of digital currency, the money will become increasingly flexible to use.

A Way to Support Emergent Technology

Technology is good for us, and for humanity as a whole. The more efficiently we can work the better for our health, well-being, and effectiveness. Thus, we are working efficiently for the benefit planet and its inhabitants.

By buying into the development of cryptocurrency, we are helping the development of technology as a tool to make our lives easier, with all the attendant advantages this brings.

It is easy to resent and reject any form of change, and cryptocurrency use certainly represents that, but by embracing it, we make it easier to spot and eradicate problems and faults.

It is a Fair System

So many of our monetary transactions, using traditional forms, are open to misuse, scams and all kinds of interference which can be devised for corrupt and corrupting purposes. Cyber currency is simple, pure, and fair, certainly in comparison to other ways of carrying out payment for trade and services.

It is, of course, also far more meritocratic than traditional banking systems. Anybody with access to the internet can bank safely and equitably using crypto currency, while more traditional systems are dependent on the existence of and access to the many large financial institutions which act as facilitators.

A Growing Variety of 'Horses for Courses'

As cyber currency develops, more forms are emerging, and this is allowing for specialization. Rather than one form of currency existing for all purposes, users can take advantage of different kinds of money forms that are appropriate for their needs. Whether it is as simple as seeking a currency that sits on your computer without using processing power, such as Ghostcoin or, for those who need total anonymity, Darkcoin.

Of course, however, there are some downsides to using this form of monetarization. Some unscrupulous people will hide behind legitimate fronts, and we must always be aware of these. As online currency systems develop and enlarge, Governments and major financial institutions will seek to become more involved with them, often looking to make their own gains from such involvement.

But these kinds of problems are no different than those that exist at present (and have for most of human history). Humanity is an intelligent species, adept at dealing with problems, and such issues as do come about with the cryptocurrency form of money use will undoubtedly be addressed. The most expert technological brains are at work in this field. Including, the brain that is technology itself.

Chapter Three: Types of Cryptocurrency and Uses: – Bitcoin, Ethereum, Litecoin and Other Forms of Altcoin

Following the introduction of Bitcoin back in 2009, some other players are now on the pitch. In this chapter, we will look at some of these in more detail.

The Grand-daddy – Bitcoin

Such is the reputation of the oldest digital currency that it can be used for as wide a range of uses as, in parts of the world. Paying for a University place, taking your partner out to dinner or even to browse and buy from the world's most famous crypto mall - 'Bitcoin Boulevard' in The Hague, Netherlands.

With approaching 50 million transactions completed using Bitcoin, this stays the world's most popular cryptocurrency.

One of the earliest transactions was in fact for the technologically amazing purchase of two pizzas. Whether they came with extra mushroom is, sadly, no more than a matter of speculation. The $30 worth of food equated to 10,000 bitcoins. Today, such a number would be worth more than $5.5 million – an obvious sign of how the currency has become increasingly mainstream and hence increased in value. Or, for the hungry amongst our readership, that number of bitcoins could buy a quarter of a million pizzas. (For this amount, the extra mushrooms should come for free!)

Bitcoin can be acquired in three ways:

- As payment sent to the seller for transactions into which they have entered.
- As purchases from an exchange platform.
- As earnings gained as a result of Bitcoin mining (we will look at this later in the book).

As the most common cryptocurrency, Bitcoin is suitable for a broad range of transactions. It is used by up to 6 million people worldwide, and it is estimated that there are over 100000 merchants in the global marketplace who will accept the currency. These are not just small scale or techy operations, although forward thinking one-man bands have gotten in on the act – included amongst the list of companies for whom Bitcoin is an acceptable form of currency are the likes of PayPal, Microsoft, and Dell.

Bitcoins are kept in digital wallets and are sometimes used to pay merchants through a service provider, who accept the coin and then charge a fee to the traders before passing on the value as more traditional currency. Merchants will also accept on a straight forward transaction using just the currency. This private, peer to peer form of trade is, of course, one of the founding intentions of Bitcoin.

The currency is especially useful as an investment to protect against high inflation. In parts of the world where inflation is substantial, such as some countries in South America, keeping savings in Bitcoin helps to ensure that rapid price increases do not compromise the worth to the owner.

As an extreme example to help to understand this, we can make use of an analogy considering the enormous inflation experienced in Germany towards the end of the second world war. Philatelists will know that a simple postage stamp could increase in value with tremendous rapidity, costing the ridiculous number of millions of marks at its height. Indeed, the cost of these everyday objects would increase so rapidly that new values would have to be over-stamped onto the little rectangles of paper – inflation rose quicker than the stamps could be printed.

In that situation, wealthy pre-war Germans, who perhaps had assets of 50 million marks, suddenly found their savings worth the value of half a dozen stamps. However, had Bitcoin been around, then the value (as happens today) would remain outside of the influence of inflation, meaning that the owners would continue as incredibly wealthy people.

However, there are down sides to owning bitcoins. Perhaps because of distrust by the public, or associations with illicit activities as might be (certainly until recently) considered by established financial institutions, the value of the currency can fluctuate violently.

Although the underlying trend is overwhelmingly upwards, the economic analytical company, Forbes, considers the currency seven times more volatile than gold, which tends to the benchmark against which currencies are valued. Even major nations such as the US and UK, whose money is a fiat currency, keep reserves of the precious metal. Bitcoin, per Forbes, can be eighteen times more unpredictable than the United States Dollar.

For example, between 2011 and 2013 the value against the dollar initially increased a hundred times from 30 cents to $30 plus, before falling to a low of $2. Then, as financial problems hit Europe, and the Greek economy created enormous global uncertainty, a rise in popularity saw Bitcoin's value reach an astonishing $266 before crashing to $50 and rising again to a vertigo-inducing high of $1242. This means that somebody is spending $3 to buy ten bitcoins in early 2011, now had an investment of twelve and a half thousand dollars. An astonishing increase of over 4000 times its initial value. However, if that same person did not sell, his investment would have crashed to a value of just $600 by the following year.

At the time of writing, Bitcoin was valued even more highly at around $3000 each.

But, as can be seen, the overall trend is very much upwards, just don't buy or sell at the wrong time!

Ethereum – the most versatile of platforms

Ethereum honors the values of Cryptocurrencies, being developed by a non-profit making organization called the Ethereum Foundation, which utilizes some of the best technological minds across the world.

Ethereum has a financial basis but exists more as a platform on which contracts can be built, rather than a more traditional view of a currency as the actual object with which payments are made. As with Bitcoin, it utilizes Blockchain technology, receiving help from all the advantages that this brings.

It takes advantage of the user to user basis of Blockchain, ensuring that there can be no control, misuse, or interference from a third party. Indeed, its primary function is to service any decentralized application.

Amongst the current projects under development or in operations are crowdfunding campaigns, identity, and personal information security systems and making supply chains more transparent. BlockApps is a project seeking to make blockchain technology more readily accessible.

It is easy to work using Ethereum. One method is to employ a browser extension, called MetaMask, which turns Google Chrome into an Ethereum browser. Another way to gain access is to use its own browser, Mist, a system that is intuitive to learn.

Ethereum has its own tradeable currency, which is called Ether, and this keeps the network going. It can be mined, as is the case with Bitcoin, and used to pay for services and transactions on its network.

Ethereum makes use of smart contracts. These are used to allow the trading of anything of value. Conditions for a contract's execution are set, and it automatically goes into operation once the pre-determined conditions are met.

Again, because they are operating via a blockchain, there can be no third-party involvement in these smart contracts. However, the overall picture of the contract can be followed by users (to help them interpret the relevant market place) while the individual position of those involved remains confidential. It is like a private political poll. Analysts can predict an overall trend while the viewpoints of people remain secret.

It is a characteristic of block chains that they can process codes, becoming platforms for various applications, but Ethereum offers vastly more scope in exploiting this than other systems. As it stands at present, it appears the only limit to what developers using the platform can achieve exists in the stars.

In part, this is because of Ethereum's creator, Vitalik Buterin, understood that most existing blockchain technologies, such as bitcoin, were developed with prescribed purposes in mind –

usually to act as a facilitator and record keeper for peer to peer digital currency transactions.

Realizing this, he set about creating an entirely new approach, without the pre-determined limitations of the technology.

Instead of needing a new blockchain for each application developed, the Ethereum Virtual Machine which underpins the technology is flexible enough to allow all programs to run on it, (given enough memory to hold the data, and enough time to execute the application).

There are downsides to Ethereum. As it works by allowing the development of decentralized applications, each of these is dependent on a smart contract code. Since humans write them, they are fallible. Mistakes can be exploited by those whose intentions are destructive, and given the nature of blockchain technology, that it is live and exists simultaneously in multiple locations, such exploitation can have a wide impact.

However, on the other hand, the platform even allows centralized services, such as loans and registries, to become decentralized and therefore safe from interference, censorship and entirely secure from hacking, despite the points made in the paragraph above.

Litecoin – Bitcoin's Younger Brother?

Very much as is the case with Bitcoin, Litecoin works as a peer to peer currency which is digital and decentralized, with no third-party involvement in transactions. It is global and inexpensive to use.

However, it offers more than just being a younger version of Bitcoin. As a more up to date cryptocurrency than its big brother, its blockchain technology allows for a greater volume of transactions. The process of exchanging currency is fast, and it is effortless to use.

The process for becoming involved is simple – users acquire a secure e wallet, visit an exchange such as Kraken to get their Litecoin. The only thing then left to do is enjoy spending or saving your investment. Like all emerging technologies, however, change and development are rapid, and users need to still be up to date with procedures.

As with other cryptocurrencies, one way of building a supply of Litecoin is through mining, which will be examined in more detail later in the book.

The currency was created by Charles Lee a couple of years after Bitcoin. It is now the world's second largest cryptocurrency. There are various sites which can supply the currency. As well as Kraken, CoinMKT, Vircurex, BitBargain UK, Bittylicious and others are good sources with which to start. However, it needs to be known that, despite the rapid growth of this currency, it is still very much in the shadow of Bitcoin. As such, it is less widely accepted than its older sibling.

This is a bit of a catch 22 situation; it will not become more established with traders until more people adopt it, and that won't happen until it becomes more usable in transactions. However, it must be remembered that cryptocurrencies are self-limiting regarding their supply. There is a self-imposed restriction on how many coins will be produced. As Bitcoin closes in on its preset limit and given the rapid increase in its value compared to more traditional currencies, it may find itself morphing into the currency of choice for just the most expensive transactions.

If this is the case, then Litecoin may well step into the void left regarding much smaller scale trades.

Altcoin – Bitcoin It Isn't

Altcoin is a generic term for all cryptocurrencies other than Bitcoin. This is a rapidly changing group, with new coins often emerging daily, hundreds in operation and several closing as quickly and quietly as they appear.

Litecoin is an altcoin, but this is one that has become established, something many of its siblings do not achieve. In most cases, altcoins are little more than adaptations of bitcoin, offering different transaction speeds or methods of distribution.

Some of the most successful of these are Ripple, BitShares, Nxt, and Dogecoin, each of which has been used in the equivalent of millions of dollars of transactions. However, unlike Bitcoin, their value against the dollar is extremely low. Even more importantly for potential investors, their value fluctuates like an inflatable dinghy awash during a hurricane. Such is their volatility in the market place that they make even the typhoon that is bitcoin seem like a veritable oil tanker of stability in the digital tempest.

Ripple – a Little Different

While Ripple follows the basic premise of cryptocurrencies such as Bitcoin and Litecoin, there are small differences. The system is still decentralized. Rapid settlement of transactions is one of its most notable selling points.

Ripple also works as a technology that offers both the currency, called XRP and payment platform for digital transactions. Therefore, it gives a service for not only its own currency but also for other cryptocurrencies.

BitShares – The New Kid on the Block

Working at multiple levels, from software to network through ledger to currency, BitShares are another example of altcoins which, in currency form, broadly run in the same way as the market leaders. Although a slow starter, early in 2017 BitShares made a break through and have since risen quite rapidly through the league of crypto currencies, to enter the first division.

As such, the platform is one that investors might consider as being worth a punt for their cash.

Nxt – Wrestling for Position

The biggest single difference to separate Nxt from many other successful cryptocurrencies is that it does not include mining as a way of accessing currency. However, like alternative supplies, it is a platform that relies on blockchain technology.

While it does have at its heart its own currency, one of the interesting facets of the platform is that it actively seeks to encourage users to create their own coinage for use. It is notable for an unusually fast block creation facility, but is a complex system, and as such, some experts feel that it is more vulnerable than many blockchain technologies, although it shares many of the strengths of this system.

Nxt started very small, with just seventy-three people involved in the first startup, who shared (relative to their own investment) all coinage. But, for those who are prepared to spend enough time researching the company and fully understanding its working model, it does offer a genuine alternative to other cryptocurrencies.

Dogecoin – the Joker in the Pack

Just to prove that techno-wizards also possess a sense of humor, Dogecoin began life as a parody of Bitcoin, but the parody has turned serious, with the company now a proper player in the cryptocurrency market.

It is tradeable with other currencies – digital and physical – and is also usable to buy goods and services. However, one of the primary uses – keeping in touch with its lighthearted past – sees the coin being employed to 'like' the work of other internet users who have accounts.

Each coin has a minimal hard currency value, and so this method of tipping for good work is low cost, but carries more weight than something in the style of the ubiquitous Facebook 'like'.

Dash – A Rising Star?

The creation of Dash as recently as 2014 sought to discuss a relative weakness in Bitcoin. The price of the digital currency rose by 100% in just two weeks in 2017, and Dash sells itself on its ability to offer even greater anonymity than other crypto currencies in a world that is marked by the privacy it offers to individuals.

Dash is also liked for the ease with which it offers instant payments for users.

The question for investors will be to work whether Dash is just a lower league newcomer on a great cup run on course for promotion, or a stayer in the volatile world of cryptocurrency.

The Cryptocurrency World

Unless we were to produce the weighty tome that offered as its best function use as a doorstop – physical or digital – it is not possible to account for every cryptocurrency. Indeed, such is the minimum life expectancy of some, and their tendency to breed like virtual rabbits, it would be impossible to stay up to date during the writing process. By the time any such book was published, its information would be as useful and relevant as an abacus in the electric age.

Hence, we have focused on just some of the biggest players.

At the end of 2016, there were at least 700 known crypto currencies. Each played their part in an industry whose market had grown to over the $100 billion mark. Knowing which of these are worth an investment and which is just an asteroid entering the atmosphere – minor flash and then nothing – is, of course, down to the skill (and luck?) of the investor.

However, hopefully, the seven individual currencies and platforms we have highlighted will offer an insight into the variety of specializations out there.

Chapter Four: Legitimacy of Cryptocurrency

One of the major obstacles cryptocurrencies have had, and are still having, to overcome is their exaggerated and misplaced reputation for being associated with the underworld of financial transactions.

Although GreenCoinX, a cryptocurrency which opts out of the anonymity most celebrate, is trying to sell itself on the fact that users' identity is needed, take away the anonymity of cryptocurrency, and one of its main benefits is lost.

The media loves a good story, particularly the tabloids and red tops, and enjoys a conspiracy even more. Cryptocurrency has been associated with everything from illegal purchases on the dark web to the funding of terrorism.

Stories and claims often overlook that the very nature of blockchain technology counts against illegal activity. It is impossible to bury transactions that the participants would rather stay secret, even though the identities of the parties are kept hidden (although for how long this would stand up to a serious investigation by an authoritative body such as the CIA is open to question).

And with the kind of figures involved in transactions these days for what is still a new financial concept, most users are undoubtedly legitimate. The extent of money laundering prevention measures that affect us all when we try to use physical currencies strongly suggests that the overwhelming majority of undesirable transactions occur using traditional monetary forms.

Nevertheless, disproving false claims is hard to do, and the cryptocurrency community accepts that this is just another cross to bear for the innovative and forward lookers of the world.

However, some of the most significant players inadvertently involved in proving and promoting the legitimacy of cryptocurrency might also offer one of the greatest risks to its future success.

Blockchain technology has now attracted the attention of the main financial institutions. Being accepted by the likes of Apple, JP Morgan, Paypal, and Microsoft means, on the one hand, that cryptocurrencies have entered the mainstream.

But, by doing so, they are bound to attract mainstream regulation and scrutiny. It is the nature of growth that when niche provision succeeds, people get to know about it and are drawn in. It then no longer becomes niche. From art festivals to technology to finance, when a niche works, people want to join it and it no longer becomes niche.

With something so volatile as a cryptocurrency, growth into a mainstream facility may put off those who are most attracted to its unusual nature. Equally, by attracting the world's major financial, retail and economic institutions, the concept may be enjoyed by all.

There will be a bit of both. Just as the CD ended the life of the cassette player, the speed and security of blockchain technology will signal the end of credit cards and traditional currencies. However, more likely is that the best bits of the technology will be adapted and employed to make these traditional banking systems better for all; or at least, the banks themselves. The creativity and left field thinking that identifies the greatest technological innovators will mean that they develop something new to become the next niche.

These kinds of outcomes can only be viewed as speculative, but what is more certain is that the big organizations are currently legitimizing the use of cryptocurrency are not there for charitable reasons. They see profit at the end.

PWC.com, a leading US financial analysis organization, believes that crypto currency will gain increasing legitimacy over time, but progress towards this will be in jumps and spurts, rather than in a linear way.

It identifies five significant parties as contributors to the growing legitimacy.

- *Consumers and Merchants*: Faster speeds, lower costs, and protection of personal information are the primary drivers for consumers towards more widespread use. However, the volatility of the still extremely small market means that consumers are still reluctant (albeit increasingly less so) to use crypto-currencies as payment tools, instead mostly using the currencies for trade against other currencies. However, merchants like cryptocurrency payments – they are effectively instant, helping cash flow; they cannot be reclaimed (as is the case with chargebacks from credit card companies) and permanent records exist for the transactions. Therefore, PWC believe, merchants will offer more and more inducements to consumers to use cryptocurrency payments, making them more widespread and thus increasing their legitimacy.

- *Tech Developers*: While much tech talent has gone into the development of cryptocurrencies and the technology to support them, even more goes into the 'fun' elements such as mining. Even though salaries for tech maestros are huge, money is not always the reward such people seek. PWC believes that a surge of legitimacy will come when tech experts turn their attention away from activities such as mining and into platform development. This will allow the creation of understandable cyber security protocols and applications which will encourage the public to make greater use of the digital provision.

- *Investors*: Many of the readers of this book will be looking to invest in cryptocurrencies. But as steady growth of legitimacy encourages more and more major investors, such as the leading banks, a surge of acceptability will follow. For example, it is one thing to report 'dodgy' stories involving master criminals or tech geeks, but quite another if the reference is made to a major financial institution.
- *Financial Institutions*: PWC seems to be implying that major financial players are ready to put their weight behind cryptocurrencies. The decreasing role of the bank as a middleman in financial transactions has been embraced in the physical world, and banks have supported the growth of peer to peer payments, for example with internet banking, gift cards, Google Wallet and Apple Pay. They are ready to take the plunge into virtual money. That many banks and other financial giants now employ experts in alternative currency and blockchain technology supports this viewpoint.
- *Regulators*: There is currently a lack of consistency from Governments across the world. From high support at one end – the European Union explicitly states that virtual currencies are to be used free of VAT; through to the US, where the approach seems to be self-

regulatory; on to countries such as South Africa, where there is little support but no law against the use of crypto currency. This goes even further to places such as Ecuador where use is explicitly banned. However, because cryptocurrencies are global, it is inevitable that at some point consistent regulation will develop. At that point, will come a surge of legitimacy. However, this may be countered by lower growth in value as legislation creeps in.

So, if PWC is correct, and there is little to suggest that they will not be, crypto currencies will become much more mainstream shortly.

Chapter Five: Blockchain

Blockchain owes its origins to the introduction of bitcoin, but now has a much wider use of technology, especially crypto currency.

What is Blockchain?

Don and Alex Tapscott, in their 2016 publication 'Blockchain Revolution' defined blockchain as 'an incorruptible digital ledger of economic transactions'. They point out that its use is not limited to just financial transactions, and that it could be programmed to record anything that has value.

Blockchain is a concept that takes a little bit of time to get one's head around. Firstly, and crucially, it is not a centrally held record of business. Instead, it is one that exists in perpetuity in a vast number of networked computers.

It is regularly brought up to date and reconciled, but this happens simultaneously on the entire network. Other forms of record keeping will update by changes being made to a central record, which is transmitted to other users. By existing at once in many locations, with updates instantaneous for all on the network, it cannot be corrupted. To do so would involve attacking every single user at the same moment.

Another, and the easiest, way to imagine blockchain is as a giant spreadsheet which is found and updated in many places at the same time.

The information on a blockchain is open to a broad public and can be confirmed from any source using the network. It is available to anybody connected to the internet.

We can use the analogy of a whistle blower to help understanding of the concept further. Imagine there is an Edward Snowden like a person who has gained access to secrets. In Snowden's case, he shared those secrets with a small group of associates to make the information harder to contradict. Blockchain goes much further, sharing with anybody who wishes to see it.

However, the difference comes when it is considered that the secrets were discovered and initially held by one person, that is, Snowden. Imagine that everybody discovered these secrets simultaneously, and as each new revelation occurs, everybody learns of it at the same time. It would be impossible to change the knowledge that is now owned by all.

Another of Blockchain's great strengths is that it is updated in real time. There is no sense of a file having extra information added, sent to another user, revised by them, returned and so on. No, in the case of Blockchain updates are simultaneously implemented for all users. Since there is no chain of information being shared, there is no point in which the data can be corrupted

That is an exceptionally powerful and secure system.

How is money sent?

Cryptocurrency is held in e-wallets. A *Private Key*, like a password, gives the owner access to their assets. Each user also has a *Public Key*, which records from where cryptocurrency originates and its destination.

While there are stories of users losing their private keys, and thus rendering their bitcoins valueless, as they cannot be used, these keys are extremely secure. This is because they are created using encryption technology, which generates almost unbreakable codes.

Why Else Is It So Secure?

Because the information held by blockchain is viewed identically by all users all the time, two considerable strengths emerge.

- No single person, institution or organization controls it
- It cannot fail at any single point (because it is always live)

Further, because every transaction is simultaneously recorded on every connected computer, there is an immediate record duplicated millions of times. Such a system is truly accountable and secure.

It is also extremely transparent – the system updates itself every ten minutes, and each time adds those transactions that have occurred since the last update. These are known as blocks (they are all linked together on the network, hence 'blockchain') and are recorded and embedded in the network. The only way of changing information is to change the entire network, and at present, there are no computing systems powerful enough to do this. Realistically, there never will be.

A further self-controlling security system also operates. Whereas, when robbing a bank, the currency taken still has value, to 'steal' bitcoins, for example, would at once render them valueless, since they only exist within the system and its records. It is a catch 22 in reverse; the only way to interfere with Bitcoin transactions is to take control of every single coin, but everybody would know this, and would at once cease to recognize them.

However, it is not just Bitcoin that receives help from blockchain. The technology applies to every cryptocurrency in existence (hundreds), or that may be created in the future.

Further, while transactions details are secure, each user's identity details are consistent, defined by their encrypted code. Their public key denotes who they are. Blockchain technology, in the form of distributed ledgers (a kind of record file stored on every computer), makes identity theft more difficult, and false identities much harder to create.

The Archetype of Decentralization

Because every user adds immediately and transparently to the record of transactions, each influence blockchain. Therefore, no one body (such as a financial institution, or Government) controls the embedded currency. With our inherent cynicism towards the new, many of us are wary of crypto currencies, feeling that they are used for illegal or undesirable activities. But crimes such as money laundering are, because of the public nature of money exchange, in fact much harder to achieve.

And this technology offers way more opportunities beyond financial operations. Imagine that it was used for record keeping. Let us use the example of planning consent. If every record were to be open to every person, transparency would be much easier to achieve. Planners could not hide behind a lack of information. Fairness – locally, nationally, and globally – would be attained far more readily.

The author of 'Blockchain: Blueprint for a New Economy,' Melanie Swan believes that decentralized networks, such as blockchain uses, will be the next big technological breakthrough.

Through record keeping on blockchain technologies, elections, corporate strategy, and political decision making could become decentralized, promoting both transparency and democracy.

Blockchain – Something for Everybody, Whether You Understand It or Not

Like many of us made great use of the fax machine during its pre-email heyday, few of us understood the technology. Similarly, Blockchain technology will simply be a part of the web which most us will not fully understand, but which will help us in the future.

It's Going to Happen

By 2016, daily transactions approaching $200000 were occurring making use of Blockchain technology. University Professor George Howard thinks that 2017 will mark the further substantial change, with a sea change happening towards the even greater use of the technology.

Now, we are on the cusp of change. The concept of blockchain technology has demonstrated the potential it holds, without really taking off in a practical sense.

However, the benefits are being seen increasingly by power wielders. The air of alchemy surrounding the technology is solidifying into practical applications.

Chapter Six: How Cryptocurrency Works in Practice- – Buying Through Exchange Platforms

You should now know much more about crypto currency, the role of Blockchain technology and the increasing legitimacy of this digital monetarization. On top of this, you should have a basic understanding of some of the different examples of crypto currency, any specific uses they have and a little knowledge about their volatility.

Now it is time to learn how to get your hands on this currency, how to keep it and how to use it.

Buying Cryptocurrency

There is more than one way of acquiring cryptocurrency, but most newcomers will make use of an exchange site. As with any financial exchange, security and safety are key watchwords. The entire world of online digital currencies embraces new, and rapidly changing technology. Exchanges available at the time of writing may well have changed by the point you are reading this. Therefore, the following three pieces of safety advice are strongly recommended.

1) Check whether the exchange offers precise data about its coins in cold storage*.
2) Are its customers happy? It should be easy to search for feedback by looking for forums online, although best to do this away from the exchange site's facility, over which it might exert some degree of control and censorship.
3) Does it appear trustworthy? Evidence of this can be evidenced in a wide range of ways that are offered. For example, to trade coins using major fiat (or physical) currencies, such as the Euro, Sterling, US Dollars and suchlike, as well as by exchanging with altcoins or (if it is an altcoin you are seeking) Bitcoin. Such an approach to assessing both reliability and legitimacy is sensible, although perhaps does discriminate against new kids on the block, which may well be completely compliant and trustworthy.

*cold storage – in the context of bitcoins, this relates to the storage of currency off the line, for example on a memory stick. Although blockchain technology seems highly secure, individual's sites and servers are more vulnerable, and legitimate exchanges will store the bulk of their digital currency through cold storage to give them added security.

The next step is narrow down the choices of exchanges you like until there are sufficiently few to properly research into them, which is highly recommended (especially for those new to the experience). A briefly detailed account of some of the more popular exchanges is given below, but as said earlier, the list is ever changing. Some other sites have been mentioned previously in this book, to which you could also refer.

It is then a case of considering how you can buy your crypto currency. The most common ways will be through bank transfer, by debit card or credit card, through an escrow agent such as PayPal or with another cryptocurrency (which is, of course, of no use to the first timer.)

Ten Exchanges To Consider (as recommended by 'bestbitexchange blog')

Coinbase – a beginner friendly US site which allows purchase with a credit card and bank transfer.

LocalBitcoins – handy because it considers all currencies, is beginner friendly and allows the currency to be bought with the bank transfer, cash, or PayPal.

CoinMama – based in the Virgin Isles, this site is both beginner friendly but also allows Ethereum to be used to buy another cryptocurrency as well as allowing credit cards for purchase.

Kraken – while not great for beginners, this large US site allows bank transfer and Ethereum.

CEX-IO – the London, England, based site trades in a range of flat currencies and allows credit cards, bank transfers, and Ethereum to make purchases. It is also beginner friendly.

BITFINEX – the Hong Kong operator is better for those more experienced in cryptocurrency exchange, and, while allowing bank transfer, also permits a broad range of altcoins for purchase.

Bisq – again, not ideal for the beginner, but this site gets a mention for being one of the more popular agents to ease peer to peer exchanges.

Coinsbank – a Scottish option, suitable for beginners and offering a broad range of payment methods.

Paxful – Not ideal for beginners, this US agent also provides a wide variety of purchase methods, including Amazon gift cards.

Anycoin Direct – A European offering from the Netherlands, good for beginners and a wide range of payment methods, including bank transfer, available.

Understanding Exchange Rates

If you wish to convert US Dollars into Pounds Sterling, then financial organizations exist to enable you to do this. However, they will set the value of one of those currencies against the other.

With physical or fiat currency, this price – the exchange rate – will be decided by some factors. Included amongst these are demand and supply (if demand exceeds supply, the price goes up, and vice versa), inflation and interest rates.

However, because cryptocurrencies are global currencies, not all of these factors exist. Therefore, the exchange rate between two cryptocurrencies, for example, Bitcoin and Litecoin, is set by the market place. In other words, the rate is decided by what somebody is prepared to accept when selling, and what the customer is willing to pay for the exchange.

A similar system exists when exchanging hard currency for the cryptocurrency.

If this exchange rate mechanism is considered carefully, it is not too different from what happens in practice for hard currency. An institution such as a bank will offer a rate to buy your dollars and give you pounds in return. Let's say, for argument's sake, the bank will exchange two dollars for £1.60.

However, if you do not exchange your dollars until you get to the airport, the currency exchange desk will know that you need pounds, and this could be your last chance to get them. While the currency desk will consider the bank rate, they might calculate that they can get away with offering just £1.40 for your two dollars.

As the customer, you can always say no. But the likelihood is, given that you need the new currency, you will accept the new rate. If the airport exchange kiosk has miscalculated, and they cannot sell the pounds at the rate they offer, they will increase their offer. This is the market in operation.

We can illustrate how the cryptocurrency exchange rate operates by using the analogy of a cup of coffee.

Alan has more coffee beans than he needs and is prepared to sell some of them.

Brian wants some coffee beans to go with his milk, of which he has plenty.

Alan is prepared to offer one cup of coffee beans for ten cups of milk. Brian does not want to give away that much milk and offers five cups. The two cannot reach a compromise and Brian decides not to buy from Alan.

Brian now visits Chris, who offers a cupful of coffee beans for seven cups of milk. Brian accepts this deal, and the exchange rate is one cupful of coffee beans for seven cups of milk.

Alan hears of this, and to sell his coffee, changes the rate he is prepared to offer to the same as the one Chris is using.

Dave, Ethan, Fred, and George all hear of this, and like the rate, so they buy up loads of coffee at that rate.

However, by the time Harold hears, the coffee is in short supply. He cannot trade at the rate of seven cups of milk with anybody and is getting increasingly desperate for his caffeine fix. In the end, he goes to Ian, who is prepared to accept nine cups of milk for his cupful of coffee. The exchange rate has increased because of demand and supply.

When it is considered that the amount of supply of Bitcoin and other cryptocurrencies are small in global terms, with demand also limited, it can be understood how small changes in either the supply or demand will be magnified when it comes to trade, creating the volatility for which the market is known.

Implications of the Exchange Rate

Because demand and supply overwhelmingly set the exchange rate, it means that investment is high risk, but offers a high return.

The next chapter will look in more detail about the process of investment in Bitcoin or another cryptocurrency.

Chapter Seven: Investments in Cryptocurrency

Investment in anything involves risk. Because gold still underpins many world currencies, is versatile enough to represent something widely held as being of value and can be used to create objects of worth, such as jewelry, it is regarded as a safe bet during times of financial and economic uncertainty. However, buy gold when the price is at its highest, and sell when it is low, and the investor has lost money.

Investment in crypto currencies is even more risky, because of the volatility of the market place. We have seen how many new digital currencies have folded, meaning that the value of investments in such currency is zero – just as in the example above, investors have once again lost their money. All of it in this scenario.

On the other hand, we have also seen that anybody investing in Bitcoin, by far the largest cryptocurrency, has earned huge returns. It is just that, over time, those returns have fluctuated. On some occasions, they have displayed almost farcical growth, followed by plummeting falls. However, over the longer term, investors have made a good deal of money.

Therefore, the investor needs to consider the level of risk they are prepared to entertain with their hard-earned bucks.

Reasons to Invest

In this section, we will consider the potential positives of crypto currencies as investment sources. Be aware, though, that the value of investments can go down as well as up.

One – the Marketplace is Worldwide

There are very few nations that ban transactions with crypto currency and as such, any investment has a global market in which to sell later. In many countries, there is no tax on transactions, and in others tax on profits is a gray area at worst. Overwhelmingly, a business using cryptocurrency is legal but free from judicial interference. Investments are unaffected by interest rates.

Two – Currency Is Inflation-proof

Again, the global nature of the currency means cryptocurrencies avoid any impact of national inflation

Three – As a Peer to Peer System, There is No Third-Party Involvement

Imagine you decide to invest in property. When you purchase your investment you not only pay the seller – which is the same with cryptocurrency purchases – but you also have the deferred costs of the seller's agent, solicitor's fees, property taxes and, potential relocation costs.

Four – The System is Decentralized

All records are stored in Blockchain, which means that they are managed by the network of the currency itself. This self-management adds a level of security by removing other parties from your business.

Five – Speed

Buying and selling your cryptocurrency is instant. There is no delay such as is caused by storage of funds by a third party. This not only invests easy but is a big attraction for people seeking to utilize the currency. Thus, demand is increased, which usually means that the value of your investment goes up.

Six – Privacy

Your investment is private. While the blockchain technology gives a permanent record of the transaction, it does not identify the parties involved. Monies cannot be traced to individuals, and cannot be reclaimed. You buy what you see, and keep what you buy.

Further privacy is gained in that the only person who can see into your account is you, through your private key and personal wallet. With traditional accounts, the institution in which your money is held can also witness the full details of your financial behavior.

Seven – The Impressive Record of Bitcoin and Other Major Cryptocurrencies in Terms of Returns on Investment

As has been regularly stated, but bears repetition, Bit has an excellent record of accomplishment of overall growth in value. Other cryptocurrencies, such as litecoin and Ethereum, have also done well.

Eight – Ease of Transfer

Because the currencies have no physical form, we can keep millions of them in our digital wallet. This means we can transfer and trade with considerable ease. It is like a traditional online bank account, but one to which only the owner has any form of access or insight.

Nine – The Increasing Use of Cryptocurrency and Associated Legitimacy

It is widely recognized that the world of cryptocurrency is growing fast. With each passing day, it becomes more legitimized, and the imminent involvement of more financial institutions will lead to bursts of further acceptability, and therefore more demand. These, in the short term at least, should result in growth in value as demand outstrips supply.

Ten – Security

The blockchain technology on which cryptocurrency is based is very secure. At the time of writing, there had been no major security breaches. Remember, as we said at the beginning of this book, the concept of blockchain is ground-breaking. There is no central record of information. All details are stored simultaneously on millions of computers, creating an indestructible system since every one of those computers would need to be hacked simultaneously to breach this safety net. Such security makes cryptocurrency incredibly appealing.

Risks of Which to be Aware

While we believe that the opportunities for investment far outweigh the risks, it would not be responsible were we to fail to point out the main dangers.

Involvement of Large Institutions

While such involvement might also prove helpful, historically, large financial and economic institutions, including Governments, tend to adapt things for their own benefit. As they become more involved in cryptocurrencies, it is hard to predict the long-term impact on prices.

Regulation

As said earlier in this book, it seems that at some point, given continued growth, global agreements will be reached with regards to regulation around cryptocurrency. This may create an irresistible 'middle man,' from which could flow associated costs, such as taxation or commission.

Failure

Despite the strength of the main players, the risks of an investment in new or smaller cryptocurrencies are high. However, these should be offset by the opportunity supported massive return. It is like backing an outsider in a sporting competition, the risk that your team or player will fail to succeed is great, but Leicester City did win the English Premier League.

Hacking and Private Keys

While Blockchain seems highly secure, individual accounts are more vulnerable. Losing a Private Key can be catastrophic – although rare, it does happen.

The Novelty of the Concept

Property, art, physical currency, stocks, and shares – these and other mainstream investment opportunities have been around for a long time. As such, relative to cryptocurrencies, prices are stable. And with stability comes certainty.

The very novelty of crypto currencies, (only around for eight years, and accelerating in growth to become widely known being an even more recent development), makes them an attractive target for investment. But, equally, that novelty means that there is little record of accomplishment on which to base an argument for satisfactory returns.

Chapter Eight: Digging for Victory- A Chapter on Mining

As we said at the beginning of this book, there are more ways to acquire most cryptocurrencies than simply buying from an exchange. Another way of getting your hands on the little money makers is by mining them. Indeed, an original function of Bitcoin was the application of mining to create a fun way of making some financial gain.

In the context of crypto currency, mining involves computer users employing their technologies to solve mathematical problems.

When successful, users are awarded the platform's currency, in the form of digital coins.

With interesting foresight, Bitcoin, was programmed to start its life with easy mines to exploit, so much so that all that was needed was a up to date computer, desktop, or laptop, run by somebody with an interest in and understanding of the technology.

However, as the coin became more and more established, programming made mining more difficult, like levels of a computer game, until, by the mid-2010s, specialist computers were necessary for success.

With supply capped and coins typically being worth $500 a piece by 2014, there had to be a significant challenge to sustain the value of the currency.

Litecoin and Ethereum, as other podium contenders behind Bitcoin's race leading, gold medal position, are still financially worthwhile to mine for the individual.

A Wide Field

Even many of the smaller and newer crypto currencies are worth trying. Getting a handful of coins today might be worth just a fraction of a US dollar, but should any of these currencies take off in the future, there is the potential for miners to be sitting on a fortune. Plus, of course, to people fascinated by technology and math, mining is a great hobby. While Grand Theft Auto or Fifa '17 might offer hours of amusement, fun is the only reward. Mining cryptocurrency successfully offers a tangible prize with a financial worth.

The Hardware You Need to Become a Miner

These days, a range of graphics cards run on your computer can help to turn you into a successful miner, for the smaller currencies at least. New coins to the market place need even less equipment to allow the miner to get digging.

Software – Windows and Beyond

While a straightforward operating system such as Microsoft's Windows could suffice, many experienced miners feel that it is not best suited to host mining software.

Security risks are quoted as a key reason the most experienced miners prefer a Linux operating system. Further, some specialist programs exist which have been built on Linux with mining in mind. One example of this is LinuxCoin.

Specific software for the many mineable cryptocurrencies can usually be found by visiting the website of that choice.

Before you start digging with your digital pick-axe, a wallet is needed to store your computerized ore. We will look in more detail at wallets in the next chapter.

If, and when, you are successful, the coins you receive will come in the form of a private key. This is an encrypted code that you store in your wallet, or even simply write down. Your coins are stored in this system, which is unique and only accessible to you.

But beware, losing the private key means that the coins are gone forever. This might not seem too much of an issue if your intention when mining is to experience the fun and challenge of discovery, but imagine how you would feel if your fifty coins, worth $0.00001 each today, take off? Three years on they *could* be valued at $100 each. As daft as that seems, remember that it happened to Bitcoin

Beware of Hackers

As with the details of your physical bank account, security awareness is critical. Hackers can develop malware at a rate faster than our guardians can render it redundant.

A virus that tracks your keystrokes will find entry to your wallet as easily as a skilled pickpocket in a crowded shop.

Therefore, the fundamental security measure of making sure your anti-virus software is up to date is as important for mining as it is for anything else. Newcomers to the system can be fooled into thinking that everything is safe because of the security offered by blockchain technology, but hackers are not trying to hack blockchain, they are seeking to find ways to your own, personal, accounts.

A good wallet will also help with keeping your hard-earned bitcoins, or other currency, safe.

Join a Team or Go It Alone?

The chances of getting a jackpot winning line on a major lottery are millions to one. For this reason, many players choose to join a syndicate. This means that they get to play far more lines, increasing their chances of glory, but at the cost of sharing their winnings with other syndicate members.

The same principle exists for crypto currency mining. Getting success on Bitcoin is impossible without the sort of computing power that is beyond the reach of an everyday user. As a reaction to this, mining pools have developed. These consist of groups of users who combine their computing power to increase their chances of discovering crypto gold. Like the syndicates, however, any finds are then shared amongst the group. Mining pool sites, such as Multipool, work by taking a small percentage of mined currency in return for easing the shared operation.

Other sites work differently; for example, Miningfield.com will allow you to begin mining for a range of currencies, and offers security services to protect miners. Since it also offers access to Tit Pool, for Tit coin mining, it certainly deserves a mention here. Rather sweetly in such high-tech surroundings, it even offers face to face advice and support through the rather long in the tooth facility, Skype.

Time To Make a Start?

And that is broadly it. As with all elements of this book, this brief overview will be enhanced by your own research. However, if you are looking at going big straight away, be prepared for an outlay of thousands, even tens of thousands, of dollars for specialist equipment. But if you are just after the thrill of exploration, or wish to speculate on significant returns from smaller coins in the future, the cost is less.

Equally, going it alone will be more expensive than joining a pool. It is all about what works best for you.

Chapter Nine: Wallets

The wallet is, in its simplest form, the object in which you store your currency. Just as your stylish leather Louis Vuitton holds your cash, which exists in tangible form and therefore needs a physical object in which to store it, so your crypto-wallet lives in digital form storing currency that likewise only exists in this format.

E Wallet

This is a generic term for any currency holder that exists only in virtual form. Therefore, all wallets storing cryptocurrencies are a sub type of an e wallet. However, many millions of us already have our own e-wallets, using them regularly. Online betting companies that can be accessed from an app on your phone employee wallets. Within them is the cash to be used for betting. Winnings are also added to this wallet, and money can be transferred to and from a regular bank account when the customer chooses. PayPal is another example of an e wallet

E wallets are a further illustration of the mysterious world of cryptocurrency being, in fact, more familiar than many of us might believe.

Cryptocurrency Wallets – What Do They Do?

In fact, these wallets are complex software programs. They store user's public and private keys, on which their actual currency owned is stored. Wallets can interact with blockchain, on which all deals have been recorded, and can thereby be used to both conduct transactions and monitor the total amount of cryptocurrency a wallet owner holds.

Then, when a person wishes to use their cryptocurrency, the keys held in their wallet link, with the buyer's total automatically decreasing by the same amount the seller's increases. The transaction has then added the blockchain.

Types of Cryptocurrency Wallet

Software – Desktop

This kind of wallet is downloaded and then installed on the owner's laptop or PC. It can only be accessed from the computer in which it has been placed. As such, there is the security advantage that nobody else can see it, but this is countered by the fact that an individual computer could be hacked or catch a virus, which might result in all monies being lost.

Software – Online

These are cloud-based wallets. The advantage of any cloud based file or program is that it can be accessed from anywhere, but this has the associated threat that it is controlled by a third person (the cloud operator) and as such could be more vulnerable to cyber-attack. However, specialist sites such as Blockchain.info offer further levels of security, sending an activation code to a mobile phone when the currency is to be used. Also, the wallets are encrypted and are password dependent. Blockchain info even offers the opportunity of giving a second password which is entered via mouse and on-screen keyboard, to render any key stroke logging malware from which your computer might be infected ineffective.

Software – Mobile

These wallets exist in the form of an app which runs on your phone. Because there is less memory space on such a device, wallets are usually small and basic. However, they carry the versatility of being able to be used anywhere.

Hardware Wallets

One of the problems with software wallets is that software can readily be attacked. Even anti-virus programs can sometimes be bypassed. For this reason, it is good practice to keep most your cryptocurrency on a hardware wallet.

This will usually be on a USB stick. Hence a hardware wallet works by making transactions online but storing coinage offline. They are flexible to use as they can be plugged into to any internet enabled device, but don't accidentally throw yours in the trash can, or let the dog eat it.

Paper Wallets

A paper wallet can be as simple as a piece of paper on which your public and private keys are written. But, don't lose the bit of paper or all is lost – literally. Another form of a paper wallet is a piece of software which creates two printed keys. With this type of wallet, an added level of security is provided, because while the public key is still available on the internet, your private key is physically found offline. It only goes online when you need to use it.

Chapter Ten: Case Studies – Three Examples of Investors in Cryptocurrency- Who Made Good

The Fall and Rise of Roger Ver

Back at the turn of the millennium, Roger Ver stood as a Libertarian candidate for the California State Assembly. Unsurprisingly, he lost. Things got worse when the fallout led him to receive a 10-month federal prison sentence – he was convicted of dealing in explosives without a license. (Per Wikipedia, he marketed these under the title of pest control. A not untrue, if extreme, way of getting rid of moles in your garden).

However, Ver learned from his mistake and, while behind bars, taught himself Japanese. After release, he emigrated to Tokyo and made himself a millionaire within three years.

In fitting with his anti-interference viewpoints, he became fascinated by the potential of crypto currency. Before long, he was almost evangelic about Bitcoin, studying all aspects of the currency as fully as he could.

He began investing in 2011 and soon spread his wings to other associated companies, such as Ripple and Kraken. His own business, Memorydealers, became the first to accept payment by Bitcoin widely. Such was his commitment that, even as a new investor, he lent his time and ability in a failed bid to restore a primary exchange agent, Mt. Gox, after the bitcoin price plunge of 2011.

Bitcoin advocate Ver is sometimes known as the Bitcoin Jesus, albeit a wealthier Messiah than the historical visionary. His net worth, much of it deriving from cryptocurrency activities, is estimated at over $50 million.

Kate Craig-Wood – a Commitment to Cryptocurrency

Like many cryptocurrency investors, Kate Craig-Wood started small. Early on, she bought 30 bitcoins from a European exchange for just under £100.

Her motivation was partly a liking for the anarchic, anti-financial institution, anti-middle man nature of cryptocurrency, and partly a business person's sense for profit.

Within a year, while the coins sat quietly increasing in value, she discovered that her investment had increased twenty-fold.

Motivated by her success, she threw herself into research of digital currencies and realized that there was more out there than just Bitcoin. She invested in a range of altcoins and doubled her money in just a couple of months.

Even more inspired, Kate next got into mining big time. She felt that even if it did not work out, there would be benefits from her learning for her day job – CEO of a technology company. Her entrepreneurial feelers went into overdrive, and she was prompted to start (with a few other tech experts) Ciphermine, which snowballed.

Sensing that Litecoin had an even better outlook than Bitcoin, Kate placed her profits in the newer coinage.

An activity that started as a hobby had turned into a real money maker. And one that offered enjoyment as well.

Kristoffer Koch and His Forgotten Fortune

This final case study is for people who choose to make a small investment into one of the newer, not very valuable, altcoins.

When bitcoins were just tiddlers in the financial world, newly born and vulnerable to all kinds of financial predators, Norwegian Kristoffer Koch spent just over $25 worth of his native kroner buying 5000 bitcoins. Such a venture would set an investor back over $15 million today for Bitcoin. But a much tinier sum for some of the newer, smaller crypto currencies.

As any of us might, were we to impulse buy a cheap pair of slipper for $25, he stored them away and completely forgot about their existence. This was in 2009.

Four years later, he read in the media about the growth of decentralized currency, run on a peer to peer basis, and he remembered his minor investment. It took him a while to recall even the password to his wallet, but eventually, he succeeded and peered inside to discover that his tiny investment had made him a Norwegian millionaire five times over.

Conclusion

Thanks again for taking the time to download this book!

You should now have a good understanding of crypto currency and can make a more informed decision about whether it is for you.

It cannot be reiterated enough that technologies around cryptocurrency are fast changing. The same applies to the range of currencies available, their exchange rates with other cryptocurrencies and their value against traditional money.

Equally, the legitimacy of crypto currency is increasing all the time, which has the positive effect of making it attractive to use, but we do not know how the involvement of the major financial organizations and national Government actions (or, indeed, continued inaction) will affect on matters such as legislation and taxation.

Go back even a couple of years, and some people who knew of Bitcoin now would describe it as dark and murky, the currency of crime, drug abuse, and terrorism. Go back just a little further, and the even fewer people with a little knowledge of the coin would laugh it off as a pointless experiment in geekism.

Oh dear. Thank goodness for the bravery and commitment of pioneers.

We know much more today. Bitcoin is a legitimate, widely used currency whose advantages far outweigh any problems. Further, it has been joined by other, newer currencies which have sought to view Bitcoin in the perspective of its life, analyzed its weaknesses and sought to offer a better alternative.

Many of these new currencies have flared briefly before vaporizing into the empty voids of the cyber-sphere, but others have survived, found their niche, and are growing well.

However, this book has sought to provide readers with a basic outline of the enormous, organic mass that is crypto currency. The strongest advice we can now offer is to reflect on what you have read, and carry out your own research into the areas that are of special interest to you. The internet is awash with opinion and information.

From that, you might decide to invest, or take up mining.

And who knows, do this and you could, one day, realize a fortune.

If you enjoyed this book, please take the time to leave me a review on Amazon. I appreciate your honest feedback, and it helps me to continue producing high-quality books.

GLOSSARY OF TERMS

Altcoin – the name given to all crypto currencies that are not Bitcoin.

Blockchain – the technology upon which the concept of cryptocurrency is built.

Cold Storage – keeping cryptocurrency offline.

Decentralization – the process by which currency operates on a per-peer basis, with no central controlling agency.

Exchange Rate – the price of buying one currency with another currency.

E-Wallet/Digital Wallet/Wallet/crypto-wallet and other forms which include 'wallet' – the virtual 'safe' in which the cryptocurrency owned by an individual or organization is stored.

Fiat Currency – Currency that has no intrinsic value, such as paper money. Most national currencies are Fiat Currency.

Hard Currency – National currencies such as the US Dollar, Great British Pound (Sterling), The Yen, The Rouble, The Euro, etc. in their cash form, for example, dollar bills.

Investment – the process of buying an object (in this case, crypto currency) to selling at a profit at some point in the future.

Market – The place in which transactions are carried out. The market helps to set the exchange rate.

Mining – the act of solving mathematical problems with your computer for which you earn currency.

Peer to Peer – Transactions that only involve the buyer and seller. No third party, intermediary or middle man takes a role.

Physical Currency – National currencies such as the US Dollar, Great British Pound (Sterling), The Yen, The Rouble, The Euro, etc.

Private Key – the unique and encrypted code that is the only record of the actual coins you own.

Public Key – the encrypted code that is used to move currency across the internet.

Public Ledgers – Records of transactions that are open for all members of the community to see.

Volatility (in the market or exchange rate) – rapidly shifting prices for, in this case, crypto currencies.

www.ingramcontent.com/pod-product-compliance
Lightning Source LLC
Chambersburg PA
CBHW050015230526
45470CB00003B/977